101 Secrets
Every Bride Needs to Know
About Buying
Wedding Attire

101 SECRETS
EVERY BRIDE
NEEDS TO KNOW
ABOUT BUYING
WEDDING ATTIRE

*by the Greatest Special Occasion and
Bridal Shop Owners in North America*

SPECIFIC HOUSE PUBLISHING
BOSTON & ORLANDO

Published by Specific House Publishing
268 Hamrick Drive
Kissimmee, FL 34759
www.specifichouse.com

Requests for permission should be sent to
268 Hamrick Drive
Kissimmee, FL 34759
(781) 608-1504
www.specifichouse.com

For information about specialty retail publishing,
contact Specific House Publishing at
customerservice@specifichouse.com.

Glossary by Sharon Naylor, author of 35 wedding books,
including *The Bride's Survival Guide*, reprinted courtesy
of Mon Cheri.

Designed by Julia Gignoux, Freedom Hill Design and
Production House, Cavendish, VT

ISBN 978-1-934683-03-3

CONTENTS

PREFACE

From the first day I went into business I believed that the most important part of my job was to make the best wedding attire available. In order to do that I needed the help of the best bridal stores and owners in the world to guide me and to be my eyes and ears into the ever changing wedding market. Therefore, I dedicated myself to help these bridal merchants anyway I possibly could. That became the mission of my business and the cornerstone of my beliefs. Over the years we have focused on both the bride and the level of service the bride deserves from the leading bridal store professionals who serve their needs, wants and desires.

In that light, we have come across one of the most innovative ideas that I have ever seen. I say that because anytime we could put the spotlight on the unsung heroes of our entire industry and every bride is important. The best part—although there are so many great parts—is that it has never been attempted or accomplished in our industry. I evaluate any idea with two key elements: Is it good for the consumer and is it good for the bridal store? This idea is good for the entire wedding industry.

When you look at it that way, you will begin to believe as I do that *101 Secrets Every Bride Needs to Know about Buying Wedding Attire,* written by the greatest bridal shop and special occasion store owners in North America, and the way it is designed, is destined to be a real winner. We praise the efforts of Rick Segel, President of Specific House Publishing, and his efforts for making this idea a reality.

Have a wonderful wedding. Learn from the professionals and consider buying one of the many Mon Cheri dresses from our family of designers and companies.

Steve Lang, President
Mon Cheri Bridals

INTRODUCTION

Getting Married is One of the Most Special and Memorable Times of Our Lives

Getting married can be the best of times and it can be some of the most frustrating times of our lives. The purpose of this book is to lessen those challenging times by giving you the information you need to become a savvy and shrewd wedding attire consumer.

There is no better place to learn about buying wedding attire than from the people on the front lines of the industry. Within this book we have created a collection of some of the finest bridal store owners in North America. These store owners have shopped the major bridal markets throughout the world and have reviewed the major bridal lines, designers and manufacturers to deliver the finest products the wedding industry has to offer.

This book represents just a tip of the knowledge of the hundreds of years of experience and wedding know how that these store owners bring to the wedding industry. They are respected members of their communities and partners in the worldwide wedding industry today. Their knowledge will help you

to make your wedding memorable and everything every little girl fantasized her wedding to be.

Enjoy the candor, learn from their advice and have a wonderful wedding day.

Rick Segel, Publisher
Specific House Publishing

CONTRIBUTORS

Elodia Adamson &
Sophia Adamson,
ELLA BLU

Juanita Bales,
FORMAL AFFAIRS, LLC

Minerva Bateman,
MINERVA'S BRIDAL

Linda Bensoni,
LADIES & GENT'S
FORMAL WEAR

Caroline Berend
BRIDAL BOUTIQUE

Karen Cardillo,
BRIDAL VILLAGE

Denise Case,
THE PRINCESS BRIDAL

Maureen Chandler,
BLUSH BRIDAL BOUTIQUE

Patti Chwasczinski,
BLACK TIE AFFAIR

Helen Dionne,
A DAY TO REMEMBER
BRIDAL BOUTIQUE

Glenda Edmunds,
A LA MODE

Jackie Ellingson,
JACKIE J'S BRIDAL

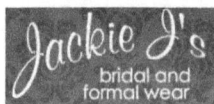

Rachel Esposito,
BEL FIORE BRIDAL

Leslie Henney &
Brion Rodgers,
BELLA DONNA'S

Jill Ivers,
MIA BRIDAL COUTURE

Shelley Kelley,
CLARK'S BRIDAL

Cathy Kuhn,
THE PERFECT BRIDE

Angela Kurosaka,
CENTER STAGE
SOCIAL OCCASION

Tanya Manatt,
BRIDAL BOUTIQUE

Judy Miller,
FAIRY GODMOTHER'S
BRIDAL

Angie Oven,
THE BRIDAL GALLERY

Aimee Pena,
SWEET ELEGANCE BRIDAL

Joy Salyards,
REFLECTIONS BRIDAL

Raquel Schuh,
BELLA VICTORIA
BOUTIQUE

Yvonne Spinelli,
BRIDAL GALLERY
BY YVONNE

Jennifer Thompson
FACCHIANOS

Stephanie Trombly,
BRIDAL EXPRESSIONS

The Secrets . . .

I dreamed of a wedding of elaborate elegance,
A church filled with family and friends.
I asked him what kind of a wedding he wished for,
He said one that would make me his wife.

AUTHOR UNKNOWN

Nighty Night
The Power of a Good Night's Sleep

by Angie Kurosaka
CenterStage Social Occasion
Birmingham, Alabama

Get a good night's sleep. On your appointment day, you will be fresh and have more clarity of thought on choosing the gown of your dreams. A restful night makes your skin look renewed and dewy. Your gown will compliment that beautiful rested complexion.

"The finest clothing made is a person's skin but of course, society demands something more than this."

MARK TWAIN

Dress Timing
Give Yourself Enough Time

by Rachel Esposito
Bel Fiore Bridal
Marietta, Georgia

- Bring only 1 or 2 people who are important to your decision making process. Too many opinions will only confuse you and not add value.

- Don't be afraid to purchase your wedding gown at your first bridal appointment. Be confident in yourself and know what you love.

- Purchase your wedding gown at least 6–9 months before your wedding—better if it's 9–12 months.

- Listen to the advice of your bridal consultant. Remember they do this every day.

- When purchasing your wedding dress consider, not only, the dress but the store you are purchasing from. You will be working with them for 6-12 months or more.

Don't Overshop
There Are No Do-Overs

by Stephanie Trombly
Bridal Expressions
Cadillac, Michigan

There are no do-overs! Don't let someone talk you into or out of what you really like and feel comfortable and beautiful in. And the same goes for other aspects of your wedding.

Don't over shop. Things start to run together and suddenly you are trying to find a gown you remember that really is a bunch of gowns running together in your mind that doesn't really exist! It can frustrate you and delay the ordering of your gown, possibly adding rush expenses.

It's your one day to not look like yourself. Be open to trying styles that you don't normally wear. If you tend to be simple and plain, you may just love how you feel in a beaded gown. If you think you have to have a fancy princess gown, try a simple gown. It might surprise you how it makes you feel.

How the dress makes you feel is as important as how it looks. Are you comfortable? Do you FEEL beautiful? Do you never want to take it off!

Understand the importance of the appointment. The purpose of making an appointment with a bridal shop is to narrow down your choices and ultimately make a purchase decision. It's not to just try on pretty dresses. Choose your shopping companions with that in mind. Will they help you make a final decision or insist you "try on this one because it's so pretty."

"A woman seldom asks advice before she has bought her wedding clothes."

THE SPECTATOR, JOSEPH ADDISON, 1771

My advice to you
is to get married.
If you find a good
wife, you'll be
happy; if not,
you'll become a
philosopher.

SOCRATES

More Than Appearance
Don't Be Judgmental

by Patty Chwasczinski
Black Tie Affair
Nashville, Illinois

- Don't judge a dress by looking at it on a hanger. Try it on first. It changes everything about the look of the dress and how you look in it.

- Just because a shop is small do not think you will not find your dress.

- Do not judge a book by its cover. Even though there may not be a chandelier or expensive photos on the wall does not mean you will not receive equal or better quality of service.

Go for the Feeling
It's a Different Kind of Shopping

by Denise Case
The Princess Bridal
Spring, Texas

Wedding dress shopping is different from any other kind of shopping. Normally we shop for color, size, the fit. With wedding dress shopping we are going for a *feeling*. At first glance, the details are important but really "the dress" is about feeling like the bride. Take a moment, center down, envision yourself in the moment. Then you will find your perfect dress.

"If you feel like the dress doesn't fit . . . it doesn't."

M. ROSENTHAL

It's All in the Foundation
Undergarments Are Important

by Juanita Bales
Formal Affairs, LLC
Sedalia, Missouri

Wear good supportive foundation garments when going to try on dresses. You will not only look better in the gowns you will also feel better! We all want to look slim on our special day and that will happen when you start with a good foundation.

Ask questions and be receptive to the sales person's advice. We are genuinely excited to be helping you plan a beautiful wedding and want you to look your best.

Never assume a certain style of dress will not look good on your body type. A sign of a good salesperson is their ability to help you decide what is the "best" look for you but also to allow you to try many different styles—even encouraging you to try things you never dreamed of trying.

It's About You
Avoid Outside Distractions

by Joy Salyards
Reflections Bridal
Harrisonburg, Virginia

Remember your bridal visit is all about you! If you have small children, you will want to get a baby sitter for the day, so that your attention may be focused on your objective: "Your Perfect Gown" for your day!

"There's something about a wedding gown — it is prettier than any other gown in the world."

UNKNOWN

Who Do You Shop With?
Pick Carefully

by Shelley Kelley
Clark's Bridal and Formal
Jonesboro, Arkansas

Be selective in whom you choose to go wedding gown shopping with you. Family and friends should be able to tune into your feelings as well as your personality and tastes, and not try to influence you into choosing a style that they personally would choose for themselves.

Be sure to make the final decision based on what you love and feel good in! If necessary, enlist the aid of the bridal consultant to "be on your side." That's what we are here for. A good bridal consultant wants you to look and feel beautiful on such a special day, as well as in the years to come when you are looking at your wedding photos.

A second word of advice: I hear many people say: "You'll know your dress when you find it." Yes, some brides do know almost immediately, but many do not. It may depend on your personality, the mood you're in when shopping/trying on, or your "shopping" style. I had one bride who came here first to shop for a wedding gown and we found one that she really liked and fit the description of what she wanted when she came in the door. However, she was a shopper and an agonizer, and worried that there might be another dress out there that was more "perfect." She didn't hear bells and whistles, so therefore maybe it wasn't "the" dress. She went to 15 bridal stores to try on (I'm not kidding!) and come back into my store to try that dress on another couple of times in the midst of all the other stores. After 3 months of hard shopping, she ended back in my store, choosing the original wedding gown that she really liked. As individuals, we all have our own unique style and mental process; so don't feel anxious if you don't immediately "know your dress." You'll find it!

*To love someone
deeply gives
you strength.
Being loved by
someone deeply
gives you courage.*

LAO TZU

Kathy Ireland

*"It is a great joy to join
the extraordinary team at 2be in serving
brides and their families."*

Mon Cheri Bridals, LLC and entrepreneur and designer Kathy Ireland have collaborated for Kathy to become the chief designer for the 2be Bride collection. Launched for the Spring 2011 season, the new kathy ireland Weddings by 2be designs include wedding dresses, bridesmaid dresses and mother of the bride styles. Kathy's longtime passion to offer practical solutions for people in love has come to fruition in the marriage of these two companies. With her past experience in designing bridal jewelry for the kathy ireland

Bridal brand as well as for numerous other collections, Kathy brings a refreshing perspective and design direction to the 2be brand.

"It is a great joy to join the extraordinary team at 2be in serving brides and their families. It is critical to me that our involvement be authentic and hands on. Our companies have enjoyed discussions for years before this dream became a reality. To offer bridal fashion solutions, we were open to only one partner, Steve Lang and his incredible organization. 2be and its related entities are strategic, deliberate and gifted in design, marketing and innovation. We believe this is a wedding that will lead to a great and lasting marriage. In the world of weddings, 2be is a wonderful place for our collections. Everyone at kathy ireland Worldwide is thrilled by this new relationship," said Kathy Ireland.

Mon Cheri Bridals CEO, Steve Lang adds, "To say I'm thrilled that Kathy has partnered with Mon Cheri is an understatement. She is one of the most influential women in home and apparel design. The kathy ireland brand has been acknowledged by Forbes as being responsible for retail sales of 1.4 billion dollars a year.

kiWW has five Good Housekeeping Seals and is one of the top 15 furniture brands in America. As chief designer, Kathy has added a breath of fresh air to the 2be wedding dress and special occasion line. Her dedication to the American public, especially people in love, is admirable and contagious. I have no doubts that this partnership will last for years to come."

Points to Ponder
Checklist!

by Leslie Henney and Brion Rodgers
Bella Donna's
Wyandotte, Michigan

- Undergarments: make sure that you bring the appropriate ones

- Shoes: bring the right height shoes

- Walk in the dress

- Sit in the dress while looking in the mirror

- Lighting: have the lighting dimmed

- Think about the location and time of your wedding

- When trying on a dress, remember that fit is important. Not every dress will fit the same. Alterations will make the dress.

- Recognize your body as beautiful in all its different aspects. Each dress will emphasize or minimize those different aspects.

- On a budget, every store has a selection of discontinued dresses. Don't be afraid to look at these.

"Every woman has a picture of their ideal dress. Anything else she buys is a compromise."

DR. JOYCE BROTHERS

No Experience Necessary
You're Not Alone — Go with your Instincts

by Caroline Berend
Bridal Boutique
Lewisville, Texas

In buying a high quality wedding dress, remember very few women have experience. Enjoy the excitement, but along with looking great, your goal is to have no regrets. Try on as many as you want. Laugh, have fun and remember that you are the one wearing it. Not your bridesmaids, mother or mother-in-law.

Selecting the right dress is only half of the battle. Make sure the dress comes in when it is supposed to. The integrity of the shop means something.

The greatest deal in the world means nothing, if the dress is dirty, or if it does not fit right, or is not there when you need it.

How to Know
Nature Tells

by Linda Bensoni
Ladies & Gent's Formal Wear
Slidell, Louisiana

On finding "THE" dress:

> "When the tears start to come,
> you know it's the one!"

~~~ ❧ ~~~

*"The dress must not hang on the body
but follow its lines. It must accompany
its wearer when the woman smiles the
dress must smile with her."*

MADELINE VIONNET

*Love at first sight is
easy to understand;
it's when two people
have been looking at
each other for a
lifetime that it
becomes a miracle.*

SAM LEVENSON

Research for Reputation
Unprofessional Web Sites Can Be Dangerous

by Minerva Bateman
Minerva's Bridal
Orlando, Florida

Educate yourself as much as you can and don't be fooled by unprofessional web sites. Do your research. Find a retailer that has a good reputation and knows their product.

Let your bridal consultant guide you through the process from beginning to end. They know the process and have the knowledge to find you the perfect gown!

Eliminate The Stress
Use Your Imagination

by Cathy Kuhn
The Perfect Bride
Rocky River, Ohio

- When you have narrowed your choices, imagine yourself in each gown in your venue. Think of how each gown will suit the picture.

- Don't stress about the bridesmaid's dresses. Remember, as much as you want to find a dress they will wear again, few of them ever will. They knew what they were getting into when they agreed to be in the wedding.

- If you find a gown you want to be married in, just buy it! Don't feel you need to look at every gown in town. The dress you want is right in front of you.

- Moms, this is a much your day as hers. You are the hostess. Everyone at the party will be wearing a dress they love. You should, too.

• When thinking of your budget, remember you will look at pictures of yourself in your gown for the rest of your life. Will you ever see a picture of the food?

• If you're thinking of ordering online, remember that you can always go back to a full service bridal salon. A dress from a website will come stuffed in a box and very wrinkled. And if there is something wrong with it, who will fix it?

"A dress that zips up the back will bring a husband and wife together."

JAMES BOREN

White or Ivory?
That Is the Question

by Angie Oven
The Bridal Gallery
Salem, Oregon

Trying to choose between white and ivory?
Have our consultant hold the ivory up to you
in front of a well-lit mirror. Then close your
eyes and have her switch to the white. Open
your eyes—let the first impression of your face
and the difference that each color makes in
your skin tone be the decider! Most of the time
you will find that some shade of ivory will
work the best.

*Marriage is
our last,
best chance
to grow up.*
JOSEPH BARTH

Sophia Tolli

"My bridal collection has two distinct
feelings: soft classic romanticism
and traditional bridal drama.
My signature style will always be gowns
with an exceptional fit and cut."

After ten years as Head Designer at Maggie Sottero, Sophia Apostolides created a new bridal collection, Sophia Tolli. With its unparalleled craftsmanship and exceptional fit, the Sophia Tolli collection provides an array of gorgeous, show-stopping bridal gowns. Sophia also created a special occasion collection for

the Spring 2009 season. Designed in the same vein as her wedding dresses, this line features the same slimming draping, fit and construction Sophia is known for. A seamstress since her early teens, Sophia grew up surrounded by fabrics, sewing machines and dress patterns. Her aunt, a talented dressmaker, handmade a majority of Sophia's wardrobe and allowed Sophia to select her own fabrics. Sophia considers this early exposure to dressmaking as the base of her informal education in fashion design. Sophia developed a strong foundation in made-to-measure design by crafting custom prom, bridesmaid's dresses and bridal gowns in her teens. During college, Sophia challenged traditional sewing techniques and explored alternative methods of dressmaking. Her award-winning expertise in fit and construction is the result of both her childhood experiences and college education.

Sophia adds, "My collection has two distinct feelings: soft classic romanticism and traditional bridal drama. My signature style will always be gowns with an exceptional fit and cut.

The Cathedral Veil
For Now and Later

by Elodia Adamson and Sophia Adamson
Ella Blu
El Paso, Texas

At Ella Blu we suggest that our brides wear a cathedral veil. It is a ceremonial occasion and the beauty of it gives splendor as the bride is walking down the aisle.

The cathedral veil is to later top the bassinet of your first born child. It makes it extra special to relive your day and dreams.

Always bring wedding slippers to your wedding . . . the last thing you need is to have your feet hurt later.

Three for the Price of One
Ways to Have the Best Bridal
Shopping Experience

by Maureen Chandler
Blush Bridal Boutique
Gainesville, Virginia

Shop early. Brides are often surprised to learn that it takes up to six months or more to receive a wedding gown once it is ordered. On average, alterations require three fittings, which can take two to three months' time. A year prior to the wedding is the best time to shop and order a bridal gown. This allows enough extra time to fix any issues that may arise without adding undue stress.

Keep your entourage to a minimum and hire a babysitter. Although it is tempting to include an entourage of friends and family in the shopping experience, it typically ends in a confused bride. When looking for a wedding gown, it is best to invite one to two trusted individuals who have similar tastes to the bride. With the exception of shopping for a

flower girl or ring bearer, a bridal salon is no place for a child. This is a once in a lifetime experience and all eyes should be on the bride.

Make an appointment with a full service bridal salon. A wedding gown is typically the single most expensive clothing purchase of a woman's life and should be trusted to a full service bridal salon. It is advantageous to schedule an appointment, especially on weekends, for the most personalized service. A bride should keep an open mind. Although she may have a particular style in mind, a consultant may pull the perfect dress based on her knowledge of the bride's shape and personality. Considering that the consultants help a bride into and out of each dress, undergarments are a must!

The Corset Back
A Step by Step Lacing Procedure

by Glenda Edmunds
A La Mode
Martensville, Saskatchewan, Canada

Allow yourself plenty of time to get dressed on your wedding day. If your gown has a corset back, start lacing it up early enough to get the fit perfect. Start at the top, working your way down. When threading the lace through the loops, thread the lace from the back of the loop forward. Try to avoid twisting the lace to ensure the laces are flat, creating a picture perfect view.

- Step one is to lace the gown, crisscrossing the lace from one side and back again. Alternate the sides when lacing; do not lace one side then the other.

- Step two is to tighten. Once again, start at the top, pulling the lace tighter through each individual loop. Do not try to pull on the lace ends, yanking at each loop. The loops will tear and the effect will be uneven.

- When you have sufficiently tightened all of the loops, adjust the bust front. To do this, the person lacing your gown will manually pull the neckline back at the side seam under your arm. This will bring the front neckline snug to your body, removing the gap. When they pull it back, place your hands behind your breasts holding the gown tightly in place while they retighten each loop.

- Once this done, give yourself 15 to 20 minutes to adjust your posture to the experience of wearing a fully boned bodice. You will find that the dress will seem looser. It is because your posture adjusts, your bust lifts, and you actually hold your stomach muscles in. This 2nd adjustment will conform the dress to your body even more.

- One more adjustment may be needed when you reach the church before walking down the aisle, simply because sitting in the car may have caused the laces to stretch.

*A great marriage is
not when the
"perfect couple"
come together.
It is when an
imperfect couple
learns to enjoy
their differences.*

DAVE MEURE

It's All in the Silhouette
The Four Silhouettes

by Yvonne Spinelli
Bridal Gallery by Yvonne
Latham, New York

When looking through numerous web sites and magazines, the choices may seem endless and brides can easily become overwhelmed. Instead of feeling lost in a sea of silk and lace...keep it simple..."The One" really is in there! The best way to find your gown is to first determine the best silhouette. The good news is that for the most part, there are only four silhouettes:

- **Ballgown:** Fitted bodice, very full skirt

- **A-line:** Fits like an "A", fitted at bust and flares at waist

- **Fit and Flare:** fitted bodice and waist and flares at mid-leg or knee.

- **Empire:** An A-line silhouette with more emphasis and shaping in bust area; often seam under bustline.

A bridal consultant will be a tremendous help to you to achieve this. If the salon provides an individual consultant to assist you during your visit, she will help you zero in on this important step at the beginning. Once you determine the best silhouette, you'll then be able to move on to the next step...the gown detail. This could be the most fun part of your dress decision. Detail can be a crystal embellished bodice, a silk draped skirt, lace cap sleeves, a beautiful sash adorned with a cluster of flowers or any part of the dress that fits your vision.

Most brides have a vision of how they will look on their wedding day. You may not have a precise idea of what your gown looks like just yet, but enjoy the dressing shopping experience. You'll soon find "The One."

Work with a Fit Specialist
Can Save You Money

by Raquel Schuh
Bella Victoria Bridal Boutique
Beaverton, Oregon

Know what styles you like. Begin narrowing down style choices. Collect photos of silhouettes styles you are interested in trying on. Having a sense of what you like gives your consultant a good feel as to what you are searching for.

Whenever possible work with a Fit Specialist. They will help you narrow down the best styles for your body type. Also, a good Fit Specialist with a working knowledge of gown design and construction can also save you money by minimizing alterations. At the very least, a good consultant should be able to determine what type of alterations you will require.

Know ahead of time if you plan on a Destination Wedding or a Traditional Wedding. This can save you time and money.

Whether you're planning a local wedding or dreaming of taking your vows on the warm sands of a beach in Hawaii or abroad will determine the style of dress you chose. A seasoned Fit Specialist can help you find the perfect gown for any destination wedding.

"A dress is more than something that looks good — it must work for the body it is on."

RICK SEGEL

8 Quick Tips
Make a Great Shopping Experience

by Judy Miller
Fairy Godmother's Bridal
Salt Lake City, Utah

1. Wear underclothing you want to be seen in.

2. Wear light makeup with hair done as you are planning to wear it at the wedding.

3. Leave children home.

4. Take as few people as possible.

5. Make an appointment.

6. Take pictures of the gowns you like.

7. Shower before shopping.

8. Be prepared to purchase a gown you fall in love with.

*There is no more
lovely, friendly
and charming
relationship,
communion or
company than a
good marriage.*

MARTIN LUTHER

Tony Bowls

*"Evening fashions have to be fabulous.
Don't just be better... be the BEST."*

In addition to his successful, groundbreaking pageant line, Tony Bowls for Mon Cheri, Tony is also the designer of Paris by Tony Bowls, Le Gala by Tony Bowls and the special occasion collection, Tony Bowls Evenings.

With twenty years of retail experience, Tony applies firsthand knowledge of what the fashion-forward customer is looking for to the designs of these extraordinary

brands. For the greater part of the last twelve years, Tony owned and managed his own retail outlet. He actively promoted and sold prom, pageant and formal-wear collections. During his time in retail, Tony also designed for Miss America and Miss USA contestants.

The Tony Bowls Collection was featured in the opening numbers of the 2006 Miss Texas Pageant and America's Outstanding Teen 2006 Competition, and on former Miss America Deidre Downs as well as eleven contestants of the 2006 Miss America Pageant. Tony has also dressed numerous contestants for 2006 state pageants, including several winners who moved on to compete in the 2007 Miss America Pageant. Tony designs were also featured on the first season of MTV's hot reality show, "Tiara's Girls". In addition, Tony's designs were graced by Barker's Beauties during CBS's "The Price is Right Million Dollar Spectacular," Bob Barker's final appearance in prime time. ABC Family's new reality show, "America's Prom Queen" also showcased Tony's designs. Most recently, Tony dressed 2009 Miss America Katie Stam as well as ten other contestants for the pageant.

Tony has now implemented his fresh innovative ideas and couture designs in not only the world of pageantry but also in prom and social occasion. The new Le Gala, Paris, and Tony Bowls Evenings collections have drawn top reviews by retailers worldwide!

It's YOUR Dress
Listen to Yourself

by Jill Ivers
Mia Bridal Couture
Houston, Texas

- Once you have found you gown, stop looking.

- Be careful of your "entourage" – listen to your own mind when choosing your gown.

- Shopping for you wedding gown should be a fun, exciting, and rewarding experience. Have fun!!

"Be careful of the advice you get when buying a dress — does someone have a hidden agenda???"

THELMA GREEN

Alterations Are Necessary
Making the Perfect Dress Perfect

by Tanya Manatt
Bridal Boutique
Des Moines, Iowa

Alterations. When choosing a dress know that alterations will be necessary and they will be an additional cost. This is your day to shine and be beautiful and what better way than to have the perfect fit for your dress. Do not think you will pick a dress off the rack and it will fit perfectly. You will need to have the dress altered to ensure that it fully enhances your figure. This is all part of buying your wedding dress.

There shouldn't be any concern if your bridal party is from out-of-town. We only need the measurements of your bridesmaids and groomsmen, and the groom if necessary, and you can purchase all of your wardrobe from one spot. This will make any last minute adjustments convenient and quick.

Formality. Honor this occasion with all the traditions and rites even though they may seem dated and unnecessary. This is your special day and while it needn't be black tie, it should not be jeans and T-shirts. Ask people to dress up for this day to participate in your celebration. Revel in the specialness of your wedding day—it's a once in a lifetime opportunity.

"Remember that always dressing in understated good taste is the same as playing dead."

SUSAN CATHERINE

*The great secret of
successful marriage
is to treat all
disasters as
incidents and none
of the incidents
as disasters.*

SIR HAROLD
GEORGE NICOLSON

The Foundation to
A Great Fitting Gown
The Important of Undergarments

by Helen Dionne
A Day To Remember Bridal Boutique
Concord, NH

The importance of proper undergarments when trying on wedding gowns or any bridal attire cannot be overstated. Undergarments are the foundation to a great fitting gown.

Long line bras provide support and lift for the bust, minimize the waist and shape the body.

Body shapers, such as Spanx, provide additional support for the body. Garments drape much better, your posture is much better and the dress fits and looks better. You wouldn't buy a new car without insuring it, would you? Protect and enhance the value of your investment (gown) by making sure you have the proper undergarments for a beautiful fit.

A Dress Is Like A Man

Choose Your Own

by Aimee Pena
Sweet Elegance Bridal
Decatur, Georgia

Shopping for a dress is one of the most unforgettable things that we, as women, do in our lifetime. We will buy cars, hones, retirement plans and more. Buying all of these things are definitely more important in life, but nothing is as emotional and unforgettable as buying our wedding dress.

So here is our advice to you girls:

- Keep the entourage to a minimum

- Choose your shopping partner with care

- **Remember that dresses and men are the same:**

    1. Looks are not everything, you need to have things in common.

    2. Before you make a commitment, date and get to know each other. Share dreams and have realistic expectations of each other.

    3. Introduce him to your loved ones.

    4. Remember you are the one marrying him, not your family and friends.

In other words, consider:

A great fit, not the brand.
Take the dress on a date, **TRY IT ON!!**

Remember that while you want to please everyone.

*"Darling . . . a dress is like a man,
you need to choose your own."*

Be Prepared to Purchase
Waiting Can Produce Disappointments

by Karen Cardillo
Bridal Village
Cambridge, Ontario, Canada

- How many to shop with—limit the number of your shopping companions.

- Be prepared to purchase. If you wait too long there can be price changes discontinued dresses, or the samples could be sold

- Be open to trying something different from your original vision—especially if you've been trying on a lot of dresses and not loving anything you've seen.

Many marriages
would be better
if the husband
and the wife
clearly understood
that they are on
the same side.

ZIG ZIGLAR

Planning Can Avoid Stress
Plan Ahead

by Jennifer Thompson
Facchianos
Broken Arrow, Oklahoma

Everything that goes on in the economy and
world affects the ordering of gowns from
weather to transportation issues; even foreign
holidays can affect delivery. Be patient—your
bridal shop is working hard to get your
dresses. Most dresses have an estimated time
of arrival. The store will call when it is there for
pickup.

You should contact your bridal shop 12 weeks
out from the wedding or bridal portraits to set
up an appointment for fittings. Bridal shops
are not alteration places so they usually require
an appointment to be fitted. Most shops want
to do more than one fitting and need weeks
between them.

Plan ahead for everything: budget, timeline for
ordering, shipping delays, or job loss. Always

leave yourself enough time. *You can never plan too early but you can plan too late.*

Plan a realistic budget for everything doing research to find out what things cost. Then sit down with your family and decide how much you can afford. When you go to a vendor let them know your budget and they can help you to stick to it.

Most wedding gowns take anywhere between 3–5 months to order so order your gown 9–12 months in advance.

Be organized. This wedding is yours and it is up to you to get things done in a timely manner.

Choose A Full-Service Shop
It Can Help Eliminate Problems

by Jackie Ellingson
Jackie J's Bridal
Alexandria, Minnesota

Respect your retailer! Find a retailer that you feel comfortable working with and value their thoughts, ideas, merchandise, and expertise. Bridal shop owners are very passionate about their stores and merchandise and are very proud of their products that they purchase for you, the customer, to see and try on. It is a large business investment to have a wonderful selection for you, the consumer, to see, try on, and look for your favorites.

The online web sites will not service you the way a bridal shop will. Look for the best service out there when planning your special day since it is a very exciting, emotional time for you and your entire party. A reputable retailer will work with you from start to finish with all of your details and help you have that perfect day! And above all, remember to have

fun and enjoy all the aspects of planning your wedding. You will have a great time and great memories!

Full service shops are of great value for you as a bride. Full service means that the shop will press your gown for you, help with alterations by a qualified staff of seamstresses, and also give you the added attention you need to make all of your dreams come true! The big box stores cannot spend the additional time it takes to keep track of you as a customer, so that is why they encourage you taking your dress out of their store the day you purchase. Full service shops take great pride in making sure you are the most important bride from the day you walk in to their store until the day of your wedding! Make your wedding special by getting that little bit of extra attention you deserve! After all, you are the Bride!

When planning a wedding, remember to keep in mind that problems do come up with manufacturers, shipping, dye lots, style changes and things that may become discontinued without notice. It is always a

good idea to plan far enough in advance so if something does come up you have time to work with the shop to make changes. Anywhere from 12–18 months is a good time to start picking out your garments, location, church, reception location, music selections, food etc. Do keep in mind that if something does change, it may have happened for a reason and there is something better out there for you! Again, enjoy all of your planning experience—it will be great!

"When I design a wedding dress with a bustle, it has to be one the bride can dance in. I love the idea that something is practical and still looks great."

VERA WANG

What counts in
making a happy
marriage is not
so much how
compatible you
are, but how
you deal with
incompatibility.
LEO TOLSTOY

James Clifford

*"The king of tradition. A romantic
visionary. A legend in the industry."*

A truly prestigious designer, James Clifford started his
formal career as a designer at the New England School
of Art and Design. Following graduation, he partici-
pated in a two-year apprenticeship at the House of
Bianchi and was then recruited by Priscilla of Boston.
During his nineteen years at Priscilla, James designed
for numerous celebrity and prestigious political weddings, including that of Julie Nixon and Lucy Baines
Johnson.

In 1980, James moved to New York City. While holding the position of head designer at Galina Bouquet, James worked to establish his own style and make his unique mark on the bridal gown industry. In 1987, James' hard work proved prolific when he joined a major bridal manufacturer. James furthered his career in September of 2004 by premiering two exclusive new upscale bridal gown collections for the Spring 2005 season: The James Clifford Collection and the JCH Collection by James Clifford. The new James Clifford Black Label Collection recently premiered for the Spring 2008 season, already receiving rave reviews from retailers and brides alike.

All three collections resonate with James' legendary vision, talent and unmistakable style.

You Don't Always Know
How To Know If The Dress Is the One

by Yvonne Spinelli
Bridal Gallery by Yvonne
Latham, New York

"You'll just know it's *The One* when you try it on." Every bride has heard this phrase from a well-meaning family member or friend. As much as that phrase is indeed true for some brides, it is not the case for all brides. If this is the case for you, you are not alone.

As much as we see brides who find "it" and are 100 percent certain of their choice, we also see brides who have become frustrated with the process. They will tell us that the process is harder than they expected. We often find three main causes of this dilemma:

1. Finding the perfect dress, but feeling the need to see "everything" before making a choice.

2. Visiting too many stores.

3. Inviting too many family/friends to shop
   with you.

Also remember . . . if you are stuck
between two beautiful dresses, you can't make
the wrong choice. But you also can't delay
deciding between the two! If you are waiting
for something to make the choice easier, you
will be waiting a long time. The longer you
wait, the harder the decision will be. You
won't be disappointed in the choice you make.
You will be a beautiful bride.

Don't put too much pressure on yourself to
find "The Perfect Dress." Often, it will find
you!

What Is the Right Color?
Rules and Customs Vary,
What's Right for You?

by Raquel Schuh
Bella Victoria Bridal Boutique
Beaverton, Oregon

When it comes to color there is more than just white and cream. There's champagne, white, cream and ivory. Whatever rules you might have heard about wearing white or ivory, all of the rules have been broken. Every vendor adds their interpretation, but the most important rule is that you feel comfortable with the color.

Buy the dress that feels right. Everything else will fit into place. Color is now going beyond white, ivory, champagne. There are wedding designers that are doing dresses in red, pink, gold, blue, and black and white which has become exceptionally popular. And contrary to every old wives' tail you have ever heard, there are black wedding dresses. Bottom line... anything goes.

The Second Wedding Dress
It's Not A Uniform

by Rachel Esposito
Bel Fiore Bridal
Marietta, Georgia

Although there are many rules about obtaining
a second wedding dress, the trump card is you.
People will tell you that you cannot wear white.
The range in fashion here is almost limitless
from a suit to even the big white gown, because
your first wedding was not that big.

*"A bride at her second marriage does not
wear a veil. She wants to see what she is
getting."*

HELEN ROWLAND

Nowadays it's hip
not to be married.
I'm not interested
in being hip.

JOHN LENNON

Buying Online
You Need to Touch It and Feel It

by Caroline Berend
Bridal Boutique
Lewisville, Texas

Before you talk about buying online, understand that purchasing a wedding dress at full
price from a reputable store can eliminate
potholes and aggravations. Yes, you can get a
great deal online, but is it really worth it?

*"If all the world is a stage, our clothing is
our costumes that create the character
within us."*

ALEXIS FRESON

Maternity Wedding Dresses
There Are No Rules Today

by Juanita Bales
Formal Affairs, LLC
Sedalia, Missouri

There are companies today that specialize in making maternity wedding dresses. You are not alone. And you certainly won't be the first bride that needs a scoosh more room.

"What a strange power there is in clothing."

ISAAC SINGER

What are the Wedding Dress Accessories?

It's More Than a Veil and Shoes

by Joy Salyards
Reflections Bridal
Harrisonburg, Virginia

So many times we focus on the dress and forget that there are accessories that can turn an average dress into a WOW. Of course they can also cost as much as a wedding gown. Here's a checklist to consider:

1. Wedding jewelry

2. Head piece or tiara

3. Veil and the way the veil is treated — short, long or bunched.

4. The wedding hat (a second wedding favorite)

5. Evening bags — never understood that one, but they are available

6. Feathered treatments, such as ostrich feathers, marabou, and sequined/beaded shawls can make the ordinary into the extraordinary

7. Gloves and garters — there are laced gloves along with the traditional at all different lengths.

8. Bridal underwear, specialty bras, bra straps, and so forth.

9. Petticoats of every variety

There are probably others but those are the main ones to consider.

Covering the Tattoo
Some Do and Some Don't
(but if it's an ex— do)

by Linda Bensoni
Ladies & Gent's Formal Wear
Slidell, Louisiana

If you have a tattoo of a previous lover or friend, you may want to consider the tattoo rescue kit that many bridal shops sell. This can cover up and erase your history. Obviously there are permanent solutions here but sometimes we just don't have the time.

Bride: A woman with a fine prospect of happiness behind her.

AMBROSE BIERCE

It's All About Fit
*Finding the Right Dress Is Only
Half the Battle*

by Aimee Pena
Sweet Elegance Bridal
Decatur, Georgia

The greatest most expensive wedding dress
that is not properly altered to the wearer
would be a waste of money. Rarely does any
bride find the dress that needs no alterations.
Alterations can create illusions of height and
cover up those extra pounds from all the
parties prior to your wedding.

"A dress is never perfect until it fits right."

MAXINE ALTMAN

*The best friend is
likely to acquire the
best wife, because a
good marriage is
based on the talent
for friendship.*

FRIEDRICH
NIETZSCHE

Ivonne Dome

"I work hard to create social occasion pieces that evoke the positive, daring feelings that everyday casual wear often stifles."

Ivonne Dome, social occasion designer for Mon Cheri, has known that she would be a clothing designer since she was a child. Born and raised in Puerto Rico, Ivonne combines ethnic details with modern trends for the Destinations, Montage, Cameron Blake, Social Occasions by Mon Cheri and Capri collections. After

she graduated from the Parson's School of Design in New York, Ivonne got her start in the fashion industry at an international lingerie company.

Since joining Mon Cheri in 1999, Ivonne has become known for her unique treatments of intricate beading, elaborate embroidery and flattering placement of pleats. Inspired by beautiful things, Ivonne enjoys the challenge of making each woman who wears her designs feel special.

Ivonne explains, "I work hard to create social occasion pieces that evoke the positive, daring feelings that everyday casual wear often stifles. There's something about wearing a gorgeous social occasion gown or suit that allows a woman to live out her most glamorous fantasies. Everyone deserves to feel special."

Where is the Focus of the Dress?
Accent the Positives

by Angie Kurosaka
CenterStage Social Occasion
Birmingham, Alabama

The dress must focus on the your positives not your negatives. If you have a big beer belly, then don't have a dress with a waistline. Is your dress working for you and taking advantage of your assets? Embroidery lace and bead work might be your fantasy, but is that really you? It doesn't have to be, but is it who you want to be?

Part of the job of a dress is to make a woman feel thinner, younger and sexier.

RICK SEGEL

What Body Shape Are You?
It's Time to Match Body Shapes with Dress Shapes

by Leslie Henney and Brion Rodgers
Bella Donna's
Wyandotte, Michigan

We are all built differently.

- **Pear shape:** means your hips are wider than the upper portion of your body.
- **Apple shape** or **Diamond shape:** means you carry your weight in your belly.
- **Rectangular shape**: means your bust waist and hips are a straight line, without much indentation.
- **Hour glass shape:** means that your waist is small and your bust and hips are more balanced.
- **The inverted triangle:** simply means your bust is prominent and not in balance with your waist and hips.

Knowing this, pick the dresses that match and work for your body type.

Redesigning or Restyling Your Dress

*Wearing a Family Heirloom
Is a Rare Occasion*

by Shelley Kelley
Clark's Bridal and Formal
Jonesboro, Arkansas

Redesigning is common when you are wearing a family heirloom dress. However, sometimes you can find a dress that is 90 percent right and might just need some additional appliques or sash. Sometimes a dress might just need gussets. A gusset can make a dress comfortable, wearable or can serve as an accent to a dress. You are only limited by your imagination and the capabilities of your dressmaker. Be careful in doing too much to the dress.

Having a Custom Wedding Dress Made
These Can Be the Best of Times and the Worst of Times

by Glenda Edmunds
A La Mode
Martensville, Saskatchewan, Canada

We are not real believers in this because you are paying a lot of money and you are not assured of a superior product. This is a practice that is not as popular as it used to be, simply because of the extent of the choices available today.

"Women usually love what they buy yet they hate two thirds of what is in their closet."

MIGNON MCLAUGHLIN

The Mature Bride
We're All Younger Than We Think We Are

by Tanya Manatt
Bridal Boutique
Des Moines, Iowa

The number one mistake that brides in this category make is trying to look like the younger bride. A strapless dress is fine as long as it looks good on you. A V-line and sweetheart are great, but the plunging neckline on a mature woman looks different than on the younger counterpart. The popular choices here are wedding suits and tea-length, special occasion dresses.

Making the WOW Entrance
Isn't That the Dream of Every Bride?

by Denise Case
The Princess Bridal
Spring, Texas

As one person said, you are already the bride which makes you the WOW. However there are some unique wedding dresses that can create the WOW. These include the beach wedding dress, the themed wedding - fairy tale/Cinderella wedding gown, the fifties style dress, and of course color is a WOW. But don't get carried away—the bride is always a WOW.

There is nothing nobler
or more admirable than
when two people
who see eye to eye, keep
house as man and wife,
confounding their
enemies and delighting
their friends.

HOMER

How Do I Find a Cheap Wedding Gown?
Be Careful — Cheap Can Be Expensive

by Jennifer Thompson
Facchiannos
Broken Arrow, Oklahoma

There are second-hand dresses, consignment shops, and yes, there are lots of wedding gowns on eBay that are advertised as pre-owned wedding dresses. If buying online is scary, then buying it this way can even be scarier. Another option are the various stores that will buy returns, excess stock, and samples from various bridal manufactures. However, if saving money is of primary importance, there are stores that are legendary for their one or two day wedding gown sales, such as Filene's Basement. Get there early, make sure you're in good shape and that you bring some tough friends to block for you.

Buying Dresses from Pictures
Can You Really Get the Feel?

by Angie Kurosaka
CenterStage Social Occasion
Birmingham, Alabama

The one important lesson is to remember that wedding gown models are all a minimum of 5 feet 10 inches tall, with the exception of the petite model who is 5 feet 4 inches tall. If you are shorter than that, the dress will look different on you.

"If you think what you are wearing is just some old rag . . . it probably is and everyone will know it."

MARLENE BARTON

Which Designer/Vendor is Right for You?
Designers Mean Different Things to Different People

by Angie Oven
The Bridal Gallery
Salem, Oregon

There are some designer/vendors that we love, because (this is not just wedding wear) they just seem to make things we like and that fit us. My experience says that when you try on a specific design that feels right, you will notice that other things from that designer will feel right as well.

Be cautious about doing business with someone that only has one or two things from a specific designer. The reason why we say that is because vendors generally take better care of their better accounts. If a store is only carrying one or two styles, they are probably not important to that vendor. This could indicate problems or issues down the road.

How Do You Clean a Wedding Gown?
Go to a Pro

by Maureen Chandler
Blush Bridal Boutique
Gainesville, Virginia

Sometimes it's more than picking it up from the store with a spot; sometimes we put the spot on ourselves. Our recommendation is to go to a reputable cleaners—doing it yourself can be dangerous.

"Clothes are inevitable — they are nothing less than the furniture of the mind made visible."

JAMES LATHER

Martin Thornburg

"I am inspired by the timeless elegance of romance, for what is more romantic than the joining of two hearts?"

Martin J. Thornburg Merchandiser/Designer started his career as a custom bridal designer and consultant. His execution of exquisite custom bridal wear was the focus of his energy and the start of a dream come true. Designing and sewing that "Perfect Dress" was a special gift. It is important to Martin to capture the personality of each bride. He focuses on designing what makes each woman feel beautiful and not look like

every other bride. Custom bridal on a one-on-one basis was only a stepping-stone to a bigger endeavor. His career has blossomed into the design and merchandising of the Mon Cheri Bridals collection.

Martin's expertise has also lead to many interviews for leading publications of National magazines such as Modern Bride and Brides as well as being quoted in various trade magazines such as Vows and Women's Wear Daily. He was also featured in an Internet "chat room" for brides to seek his advice. The Mon Cheri Bridals collection is as diversified and unique as the brides themselves. Martin truly believes that a great dress is all about shape, fit and construction. The icing on the cake is the detail and fabrics that he is so passionate about, and will not stop designing until they are perfect! The blend of these key ingredients makes a bride beautiful!

When a wife
has a
good husband
it is easily seen
in her face.

GOETHE

What's Your Shopping Plan?
Budget Your Time and Don't Skimp on This Once in a Lifetime Experience

by Karen Cardillo
Bridal Village
Cambridge, Ontario, Canada

Before you go out shopping, have an understanding of what you want to accomplish before you shop.

- Are you shopping to get ideas?
- Are you shopping to buy?
- Are you shopping to impress your mother-in-law?
- Are you shopping to revisit things you have seen before?
- Are you shopping to evaluate the various treatments a dress may have?
- Are you shopping to evaluate different vendors?
- Are you shopping to find the right store?

Have a plan and stick to it.

What Price Range Should I Be Looking At?

It's All About Priorities

by Elodia Adamson and Sophia Adamson
Ella Blu
El Paso, Texas

Here are the basic wedding gown price ranges:

- Lower price dresses are considered by bridal vendors as dresses in the $350–$500 rang.
- A better brand collection would go from $700–$2000
- The designer bride is in the $2000–$5000 range
- The extravagant budget goes above the $5500 range

The question is would a $6000 dress be any better than a $2000 dress? The answer is rarely, however, the more expensive dress comes with a more prestigious label.

Is the Mother of the Bride Different than the Mother of the Groom?
Not When It Comes to Dresses

by Jill Ivers
Mia Bridal
Houston, TX

There are 2 answers here:

- As far as the dress itself, no.

- The difference between the two people is that one of them is paying for the wedding. Look-wise it is about the same. Or as one person said, just look appropriate and keep writing checks.

Are Second Weddings Treated Differently?

Of Course They're Not the Same

by Cathy Kuhn
The Perfect Bride
Rocky River, Ohio

There is a whole category for bridal gowns for second wedding because of the popularity of them. Every bridal vendor today designs for second weddings. It is not an afterthought; it's a major category for both retailers and vendors.

"Adornment is never anything except a reflection of the heart."

COCO CHANEL

What is the Most Important Thing Every Bride Needs to Know?
Something That is Most Often Overlooked

by Stephanie Trombly
Bridal Expressions
Cadillac, Michigan

Shhhh — undergarments. The best fitting dresses generally have the best fitting and appropriate undergarments. A white dress with a red thong shining through can focus the entire wedding into something you might not want the focus on.

"Unmentionables – those articles of ladies apparel that are never discussed in public except in a full page illustrated ad."

CHANGING TIMES

When to Shop

Lack of time causes stress! Give yourself plenty of it, shop early.

by Jill Ivers
Mia Bridal Couture
Houston, Texas

If you want to reduce stress in the buying process, avoid Saturdays and early evenings. Many stores will limit your time with your salesperson, only adding additional frustration.

"The first purpose of clothes was not warmth or decency but ornament . . . among wild people we find tattooing and painting came prior to clothes. Clothes still serve that same purpose."

THOMAS CARLYLE

Appointments
If We're Budgeting Our Time —
Appointments Are Key

by Helen Dionne
A Day to Remember Bridal Boutique
Concord, NH

Yes, calling for appointments is important, but
more important is making sure that the store
you are doing business with honors their
appointments. Call first.

"Fashion is architecture — it is a matter
of proportions."

COCO CHANEL

Decide on What's Essential:
Write down the most important things to do

by Karen Cardillo
Bridal Village
Cambridge, Ontario, Canada

Whether you have known what you wanted in a wedding dress since you were a little girl or have no idea, come up with a list of things that you absolutely cannot do without and will not compromise on. Dreamt of having a long train? It goes on the list. Hate beads with a passion? They're out. This is your dress and no one else's, after all.

"One should either be a work of art or wear a work of art."

OSCAR WILDE

It Takes Longer Than You Think

Give yourself plenty of time, plan ahead.

By Rachel Esposito
Bel Fiore Bridal
Marietta, Georgia

Allow six months to have your wedding dress made, altered and whatever else you need done to it. Start shopping even earlier so there's no rush and less stress. Of course there are always places that will have some dresses in stock for sale but don't plan on it and remember you run the risk of buying a dress that 40 other brides had tried on.

A wedding is a party and sometimes we forget that.

UNKNOWN

Do You Have Any Idea of What You Plan to Spend?

Are you ready for sticker shock?

by Angie Oven
The Bridal Gallery
Salem, Oregon

There are dresses at all different price levels. There are some people who feel that unless you spend $2,000 you're buying a rag. That's just not so. Before you create a budget, get a feel for the range of prices and then budget the price of the dress. Before you say you're going to stick to the budget, understand you might just fall in love with something above the budget. That's why you should buy your dress first and then cut back on something else. Just think of how many pictures will be taken and how long you will have those pictures.

Ultimately the bond
of all companionship,
whether in marriage
or in friendship,
is conversation.

OSCAR WILDE

Joan Calabrese

"I feel the same as Winston Churchill who said, 'I can be easily satisfied with the very best.'"

Born into a family of Italian artisans and raised in Philadelphia, Joan Calabrese showed a complete love of fashion from a very early age. Joan adds, "From the day I could pick up a pencil, I was always drawing, always clothing." As a small child, Joan also sewed her own dolls' clothing, collecting fabric scraps from a family friend and dressmaker. As a high school student, she was offered a full scholarship to the prestigious Academy of Fine Arts in Philadelphia but turned it

down to work at home with her family. As a mother of two young daughters, Joan decided to pursue her innate talent of creating children's clothes.

These new designs caught the eye of Tom Morotta, Vice President of Saks Fifth Avenue Couture, who introduced her work to the prestigious Children's Boutique in Philadelphia. The owner, Linda Berman immediately placed an order for forty dresses which Joan crafted in her basement studio. It was not long before other stores including Bergdorf Goodman and Neiman Marcus also placed large orders, thus laying the foundation of a successful business since 1975.

Known for her use of exquisite fabric and detail along with pristine lines, Joan's work is considered the finest representation of children's couture. Attending fabric shows in Paris twice a year, Joan draws inspiration from European fashion as well as from couture fashion publications. Fine fabrication has always been of the utmost importance to her. "If I love it, I'll buy it. I just listen to my soul," explains Joan. The Metropolitan Museum of Art accepted two of Joan's designs for the Permanent Collection of their Costume Institute. She

is also installed in the Costume Collection of the Philadelphia Museum of Art. Internationally recognized, Joan's dresses have been worn by young members of the British Royal Family, daughters of many Heads of State as well as numerous celebrity children.

Joan joined Mon Cheri Bridals, LLC in 2008 to create a new children's collection, Joan Calabrese for Mon Cheri. Her premiere collection for Mon Cheri offers moderate prices while still providing the signature style and fine fabrication her design is known for. Classic and timeless with an edge, this collection includes special occasion, flower girl and First Holy Communion designs. Joan Calabrese for Mon Cheri is available at both exclusive bridal salons and children's boutiques worldwide. Joan's higher end collection, Joan Calabrese, will continue to be a separate entity from Joan Calabrese for Mon Cheri.

What Should I Look For In a Wedding Dress?

What kind of impression do you want to make walking down the aisle?

by Jennifer Thompson
Facchianos
Broken Arrow, Oklahoma

Traditional? Conservative? On the edge? Fashion forward? The focal point of the wedding? Do you plan on dancing up a storm? If so sleeveless and comfortable may be the way to go. The one key element never to forget is to make it comfortable. The last thing you need in a wedding is to have a dress digging in.

"No, first, know who you are and then adorn yourself accordingly."

EPIC TETUS

What's Right for You?

Every dress is designed for specific body types

by Raquel Schuh
Bella Victoria Bridal Boutique
Beaverton, Oregon

Make sure your body type matches the dress. Not every kind of dress will look good on you. Big puffy sleeves and ball gowns aren't for everybody, just as dresses with slits up the sides are set aside for certain body types and attitudes. Find a dress style that suits your body type and attitude. Good salespeople at quality stores will direct you and make appropriate recommendations. Their reputation is on the line as well.

Getting Another Opinion

This can be one of the most aggravating and dangerous parts of the entire process of selecting dresses

by Jackie Ellingson
Jackie J's Bridal
Alexandria, Minnesota

Some people say to just ask an honest friend's opinion. It sounds good in theory but too many times friends will judge dresses not from your perspective but from their own perspective. It's a wonderful gesture to invite the future mother-in-law to go shopping with you. First they will be flattered and second their motivation, as strange as it may sound, could be the most honest because your own mother is concerned about the budget. Your friends are thinking about themselves. While that all may be true, the future mother-in-law wants her son to marry a beautiful bride. I realize there are people groaning now but it can be one of the most helpful opinions!

*As for his secret
to staying married:
"My wife tells me
that if I ever
decide to leave,
she is coming
with me."*

JON BONJOVI

Do I Have to Wear White?
Only if you want to

by Tanya Manatt
Bridal Boutique
Des Moines, Iowa

Traditions change. White is not the requirement it was years ago. Even brides who are 8 months pregnant are wearing white. The tradition was to wear white on your wedding day, but if you don't look good in white, don't wear it. Off white, ivory or muted white dresses are becoming very popular and accepted. If your attitude is to be bold, vibrant and different go for it. Just remember the old aunts may be talking about you.

"Just because you love the color does not mean the color loves you."

RICK SEGEL

The Bride Wore Two Dresses
Crazy? It's getting popular.

By Glenda Edmunds
A La Mode
Martensville, Saskatchewan, Canada

A current trend that's gaining in popularity is the bride buying a sophisticated cocktail dress to slip on after dinner for the partying/dancing part of the night. This is usually the time the bride changes her shoes or just takes them off. As radical as this may sound don't worry about it because all of the know-it-all little old ladies will be long gone before the band starts to crank up. This is a great idea that makes a lot of sense.

"After all there is something about a wedding-gown prettier than in any other gown in the world."

DOUGLAS WILLIAM JERROLD

Your Photographer Is a Resource
Who would have thought?

by Caroline Berend
Bridal Boutique
Lewisville, Texas

Ask your photographer to look at some of the pictures that will be taken to simply get ideas on all types of wedding apparel. The reason for that is that you can see how various styles will look on real people. This is especially helpful if you're a more challenging body type or size. Many times the photographers can direct you from a very objective point of view because they are the one person who will be analyzing the person and the dress closer than anyone else. Not only when they take the picture but this will also come into play when they are analyzing the proofs and also when they are selecting the final selection of pictures.

Do Not Buy a Dress In the Hope That You Will Lose Weight

It sounds good but rarely works . . . sorry

by Jackie Ellingson
Jackie J's Bridal
Alexandria, Minnesota

That will only stress you and ruin the fun of preparing for your wedding day. There are too many horror stories about brides who insisted that they will lose weight and in turn gained weight with all the parties and excitement. It not only adds additional stress to the bride but the bridal shop tries so hard to do the right thing and gets needlessly criticized by trying to give honest advice. To quote Jack Nicholson "Some people can't handle the truth."

"It Will Only Look Better With the Right Undergarments"
Everyone has something to cover

by Shelley Kelley
Clark's Bridal and Formal
Jonesboro, Arkansas

This may be true but why guess at how it is going to look? Put on the under garments that you are going to wear on the day of the wedding. Chances are everything will be better with the right under garments but on a day that is so important, why risk it? A special made to order corset can make a dramatic difference to your shape. Be careful not to do anything too drastic. Shrinking your waist 2 inches is acceptable but squeezing yourself more than that could cause bruising, fainting because of the lack of oxygen or just feeling totally uncomfortable on the most important day of your life. Of course, going back to the bridal suite with a custom made corset can add an additional sense of pleasure because you can't wait to get it off.

Trying On a Dress Means More Than Standing in Front of a Mirror

Try sitting down, walk in the dress.

by Aimee Pena
Sweet Elegance Bridal
Decatur, Georgia

You're not going to dance at the bridal shop but stretch your arms a little just to get a feel of how the dress is going to react. Are you noticing any unsightly bulges especially when you're sitting down? Remember the key operative word is still comfort. If you're comfortable you will glow. A beautiful dress with a frown or pained look is not a beautiful dress because it takes away from the total look.

*Love seems
the swiftest
but it is
the slowest
of all growths.*

MARK TWAIN

The Informal Wedding Dresses and the Plus Size Brides
A marriage made in heaven . . .

by Denise Case
The Princess Bridal
Spring, Texas

Informal wedding dresses are used for garden weddings, second weddings, beach weddings and destination weddings. They are generally a simpler and easier style to wear and the fabrics are more flexible than the traditional wedding gown fabrics. That is the perfect combination that bodes well for the large sized bride. Many times these informal dresses become acceptable for more formal ceremonies as traditions change and where comfort has become a powerful reason to buy.

How Long Does it Take to Order Bridesmaids Dresses?
Longer than you think but
less than you expect

by Elodia Adamson and Sophia Adamson
Ella Blu
El Paso, Texas

Bridesmaids' dresses take a little less time than a wedding gown, but you should plan on a minimum of four months to place your order. There are some manufacturers who require even more time. Check with your store before you fall in love with any dresses. The real issue in timing with bridesmaids is getting all of the bridesmaids into the store once they are received. This is not an easy task because of people's schedules and distances. Try to work with your bridesmaids to get a commitment of time so that you can avoid unnecessary hassles or problems.

How Long Does it Take to Order Mother's Dresses?

Not long if you're buying it off the rack

by Yvonne Spinelli
Bridal Gallery by Yvonne
Latham, New York

Mother-of-the bride dresses are in a different category. Many of these dresses are sold off the rack. However, the delivery time if they need to be ordered, is less than two months. Even mothers should start getting an idea a minimum of four months before the wedding. There is a difference between getting ideas and shopping. Becoming aware gives you direction while shopping is interpreting those ideas and making commitments.

An Empire Waist Dress is One of the Most Popular and Versatile Styles to Choose from

It covers up so many sins

by Joy Salyards
Reflections Bridal
Harrisonburg, Virginia

An empire waist is defined by the placement of the waistline, which is above the normal waistline and below the bust. The reason for the popularity is because it is flattering on so many people. For women with a small bust it makes them look fuller. For women with a belly it covers the belly (great for the pregnant bride). The other major benefit is the depth of selection offered in empire style dresses from sleeveless to long sleeve, from straps to strapless to spaghetti straps. The empire dress is a classic that works for almost every body type.

Let's Talk about the Tea-Length Dress

Never wear a tea-length dress to a tea party

by Helen Dionne
A Day to Remember
Concord, New Hampshire

The tea-length dress is gaining in popularity for wedding dresses and has reached an acceptance for bridesmaids and mother's dresses for a long time. The debate is always what is the proper length for a tea length dress? It is defined by most wedding designers as a length that falls between the knee and the ankle. Be careful, this is a hot topic because there are people who will insist that a tea length dress is an ankle length dress. It is that but it can be higher as well. One word of caution is that a bridal dress that is an ankle length dress generally indicates a less formal wedding.

The Classic Bridesmaid's Line Is "You will be able to wear the dress again."

It's rare but it does happen

by Rick Segel
Rick Segel & Associates
Kissimmee, Florida

This is a line that has been around for years. The problem is very few bridesmaids dresses are ever worn again. However, there are more and more special occasion dresses or cocktail dresses that can make great bridesmaid dresses as well. Don't worry that your bridesmaid isn't going to be able to wear the dress again – they are fully aware of that and that is part of the commitment a bridesmaid makes when asked to be a bridesmaid.

A happy bridesmaid makes a happy bride.
THE BRIDESMAID, ALFRED TENNYSON, 1836

Let the Red Carpet Be Your Guide

Celebrities set the trend

by Rick Segel
Rick Segel & Associates
Kissimmee, Florida

We are fascinated by the dresses celebrities wear specifically on the red carpet. That has become the new standard for the most popular special occasion dresses. That's not new — what is new is that these dresses are now being used as non-traditional bridesmaid dresses. Then again, what is traditional today? Dresses that we see on TV, in movies and in the news become the fashion of the day. There are more manufacturers who have copied Kate Middleton's sister's dress (Pippa) than even the princess' dress. Not only did it look smashing but it was on TV for the world to see. When Princess Diana got married every designer had to add leg-o-mutton sleeves because every bride wanted to look like Princess Di. Just remember to make sure the dress looks good on you and let those styles inspire you but not control or confine you.

I got gaps;
you got gaps;
we fill
each other's gaps.

ROCKY

Glossary of Terms

"When it's over, I want to say: all my life I was a bride married to amazement. I was the bridegroom, taking the world into my arms."

MARY OLIVER

Gown Silhouettes

A-line/Princess
Narrow at the bodice, with vertical seams that flow right down to a slightly flared-out skirt.

Asymmetrical
The bottom of the skirt, as well as perhaps several layers of fabric comprising the skirt, is cut on a diagonal angle.

Ballgown
A fitted bodice that comes in at the waist and then flares out to a full, floor-length skirt with lots of volume for a more formal and traditional bridal look.

Column
A fitted bodice to a narrow, tailored look over the waist and hips, and straight to the floor. No flares, no poofs, and not as fitted as a sheath. You can do floor-length, or shorten it to calf-length for a less formal wedding.

Empire
A Victorian-style of gown, this one features a fitted bodice with a skirt that starts right at the base of the chest and hangs down in a straight, slim line to the floor.

Mermaid
Form-fitting from the chest to a tiny waist, over the hips and then down to the knees, where fabric flares out in dramatic fashion like a mermaid's tail.

Sheath
A close, form-fitting dress from bodice all the way down to the skirt. May have a slit at the legs for easier walking.

Gown Lengths

Ankle-length
Reaches right to your ankles, hemmed to a flattering point with the shoes you'll be wearing.

Ballerina
A full skirt that extends to just above the ankles.

Floor length
The skirt reaches just to the floor, the hem extended for a gentle glide obscuring the view of your shoes.

Intermission
Also cocktail length, this one reaches to anywhere between the knees and the ankles, with the most common length being mid-calf.

Hi-low
A dual-level dress, the front of the skirt is Intermission length, then extends gradually lower along the sides down to floor length in the back.

Knee-length
The skirt reaches to or just below the knee.

Miniskirt
The skirt reaches 2-4 inches above the knee.

Street length
The skirt reaches an inch or two below the knee.

Tea-length
Also called a cocktail-length dress, the skirt reaches to mid-shin.

Skirt Styles

Ballgown
Fitted at the bodice and waist, and then the skirt poufs out into a bell shape.

Flared
Fitted at the waist, and then flares out into a tulip shape at the hem.

Flounce
A looser skirt that flares out and has a ruffle at the hem.

Front slit
A slit on a frontal side seam, usually along the leg and not in the middle, that allows for movement.

Pannier
Fabric draping on both hips as an extra layer to accent a more sheath-style dress.

Pencil
Skirt hangs straight down, with no flare at the hem or accent at the waist.

Peplum
A very short ruffled skirt layer over a pencil skirt, originally a 1940s style of fun skirt with a bit of flair and movement for dancing. The ruffled layer may be horizontal in shape or extended down in a back V-shape.

Pleated
Varying numbers of pleats running vertically most often along the front of the skirt, but may also extend fully around the skirt. Multiple pleats is called 'accordion style' and two larger pleats is called 'box style.'

Side slit
A slit at the side of the leg, allowing for movement.

Straight
The skirt extends straight down, with no flare at the hem. A longer version of the pencil skirt, this skirt might reach to the floor.

Tiered
The skirt is comprised of several overlapping layers of different lengths, usually three layers, but may be more depending on style.

Wrap
The skirt overlaps and wraps at the waist, a more informal style ideal for destination weddings and bridesmaid dresses.

Bodices

Asymmetrical
The fabric covers one shoulder, or attaches over one shoulder with a strap, leaving the other shoulder bare.

Corset
Hugs tight against the body with hook, snap or laced back securing. The bodice can be strapless or strapped, criss-cross strapped or braid-strapped.

Empire
(pronounced ahm-peer) – Fitted at the chest, then fabric hangs straight down under the bustline for a *Shakespeare in Love* look. A very romantic look, and one favored by pregnant brides and bridesmaids.

Midriff
Reaches just down to below the ribs, baring your stomach.

Princess-line
Lined with two vertical seams that angle over the breastline down to the hem.

Surplice
Fabric is crossed in the front or the back, sometimes twisted for extra effect.

Tank
Just like a tank top, this one is sleeveless with thin or thick straps.

Necklines

Bateau
Straps are at mid-shoulders with the fabric reaching in a gentle dip across the chest and back, like an eye shape if viewed from above.

Halter
Like a halter top or bikini top, it ties around the back of the neck. The front might be plain or with a keyhole opening.

High collar
The chest and base of the neck are covered by fabric. Sometimes a high collar is accented with a keyhole cutout at the chest through which a piece of jewelry shows.

Jewel
A rounded neckline sitting at the base of the throat.

Off-the-shoulder
The shoulders and collarbone are bare, with fabric wrapping around the upper arms.

One-shoulder
The neckline angles up toward the one shoulder that features a strap, with the other shoulder bare.

Portrait
Off-the-shoulder, with the neckline scooping down into a more rounded cut.

Queen Anne
With shoulders covered and a high back, the front is shaped like the bottom of a heart.

Sabrina
See bateau, but starts two inches higher for a more demure look.

Scoop
A rounded neckline, like the bottom half of a circle.

Strapless
No straps. The neckline can go straight across, or dip down in a curved design.

Square
Your straps come straight down to a vertical line of fabric across your chest, presenting a square shape.

Sweetheart
Rounded fabric over each breast, meeting in a V-neck point in the middle. Its heart shape is the basis for its name.

V-neck
The fabric extends downward in an angled V-shape at the top of the chest or lower to show some cleavage.

Sleeves

Balloon
Full, round and balloon-shaped over the shoulder and upper arm, then narrowing over the lower arm and wrist.

Bell
Fitted over the bicep and then flares slightly outward (like a bell) over the forearm. This detail adds interest and something special to a simpler, classic and unadorned gown.

Bishop
Puffs a bit at the shoulder, then expands fuller over the arm, then gathers at the wrist. A very casual and natural look.

Cap
A short extension to a sleeveless look, offering a 'pouf' of fabric over the shoulder, gathering under or against the very top of the arm.

Dolman
Also termed the 'batwing' style, the fabric begins very wide at the ribcage or waist, then narrows at the wrist.

Fitted point
The long, fitted sleeve extending to a point-shape at the wrist or top of the hand.

Gauntlet
A pouf at the top of the arm, then a separate section that covers the entire arm, coming to a point at the top of the hand. The bottom section may be a full-length glove for removal later.

Gigot
A large, round pouf over the shoulder, then narrowing over the arm to encircle the wrist.

Illusion
Sheer netting-type material that forms a see-through sleeve yet offers 'the illusion' of coverage. If you're not happy with your upper arms, this type of sleeve may be for you.

Juliet
A full sleeve extending down to the wrist, with a 'puff' accent at the shoulder and upper arm.

Off the Shoulder
Wraps across the upper arms, leaving the shoulders bare.

Petal
The short sleeves are made of two to three different panels that overlap to look like a tulip in bloom.

Poet
Fitted close over the upper arm, and then flares out widely from the elbow, with long ruffles at the wrist length. It's called the 'poet,' because it's reminiscent of the Shakespearean era. This sleeve has a heritage feeling, movement and flow, and is a romantic accent to a traditional gown.

Pouf
A larger cap sleeve, ending lower on the arm.

Spaghetti straps
A strapless dress is held up by a skinny strap or fabric band over each shoulder.

Tee shirt
Extending three to four inches below your shoulders, this sleeve type resembles the traditional tee shirt sleeve cut.

Three-quarter
Extending from the shoulder to mid-forearm.

Tulip
A petal-shape, with several flaps of fabric overlapping to resemble a flower. Also called the 'criss-cross sleeve.'

Trains

Brush
Reaches just to the floor beneath your dress hem, 'brushing' the floor as you walk. This style works with virtually all wedding types as it can be formal to less formal, appropriate for outdoor weddings for its lack of drag, and fine for beach weddings. Brides say they can move most easily in a train of this type. Walking, turning and moving is not a problem during the ceremony, and they're happy not to have to carry around six pounds of bustled fabric all night.

Castillion
A French-inspired, very long train, often over 10 feet long.

Cathedrale
Attached at the waist and extends dramatically 6-8 feet behind the gown, as the train of choice for many ultra-formal weddings.

Chapel
A formal to semi-formal style, the chapel train attaches at the waist and extends 3-4 feet behind the gown.

Court
A short and maneuverable train, the court attaches at the waist and extends behind you for 1-2 feet.

Royal

Also known as the 'Monarch' train, since it has been used in royal weddings such as the late Princess Diana's. An ultra-formal style, the royal train extends ten feet or more from its attachment position at your waist.

Semi-cathedrale

Extending for a length of 5-7 feet behind the dress, this semi-formal to formal train is a mix of chapel and cathedrale-length.

Watteau

Attaches at your shoulders or the top of your back (yes, like a cape) and falls most often to the bottom hem of your dress, but may also be designed to reach just a little bit beyond the hem.

Fabrics

Batiste

A lightweight cotton fabric, in a thin grading to be almost transparent.

Brocade

A fall and winter appropriate woven fabric, heavier in weight with raised floral or ribbon design.

Charmeuse
A lightweight, semi-satin fabric known for its softness, as a blend of silk or rayon.

Chiffon
A very soft, delicate fabric in silk or rayon, extremely sheer and thus often layered for modesty.

Crepe
A thin, lightweight fabric with a rippled texture compared to a citrus fruit, often in silk or polyester.

Crepe de Chine
A version of crepe made from silk and featuring tiny bumps as texture in the fabric.

Damask
A lighter-weight silk, linen, cotton, or synthetic fabric featuring woven patterns of fruit, flowers, or other motifs.

Duchesse Satin
A light blend of silk and rayon (or polyester) that resembles a satin finish.

Dupioni
Most often 100% silk, a thicker, shinier version of shantung.

English net
Not to be confused with tulle, this netting is softer and has a bit of stretch to it.

Faced satin
A soft version of satin, made from 100% silk.

Gabardine
A firm fabric with a diagonal pattern to the stitching.

Georgette
A sheer, light blend made of polyester or silk with a less-than-smooth, non-shiny texture by design.

Illusion
Sheer, thin netting often used for sleeves and as a modesty cover for décolletage.

Jersey
A very soft knit fabric, most often 100% cotton as an informal fabric at weddings.

Moiré
A heavy silk taffeta with a wavy pattern, as well as a watermark pattern woven into it.

Organdy
Sheer and transparent, but firmer and stiffer than other fabrics.

Organza
A stiffer, heavier version of chiffon, popular for skirts due to its flowing nature.

Peau de Soie
A soft silk which is actually a heavier, non-shine satin with slight ribs and texture.

Rayon
A step below silk, with a bit more stretch.

Satin
A smooth fabric with lots of shine, woven from silk or polyester, with notable shine on one side of the fabric and a duller texture on the underside.

Shantung
Woven from silk, shantung resembles dupioni, but it of a much lighter weight and texture.

Silk
The most popular fabric for wedding dresses, with softness and shine.

Silk Gazar
A layered silk organza, often in four layers.

Silk Mikado
A heavier, thicker form of blended silk, often a choice for cooler-weather weddings.

Taffeta
Thicker fabric with movement, with slight ribbing in the weave.

Tulle
Silk, nylon, or rayon semi-sheer netting, most often seen in veils and crinolines.

Velvet
A thick, soft fabric with a short, felted pile and may be made from silk. Velvet with more of a matte or patterned design may be crushed velvet.

Laces

Alencon
A popular, delicate design of lace including images of flowers and arches on netting, with the edges embroidered with or without accenting such as beading.

Battenberg
Floral or geometric designs created by forming loops of linen connected by threadwork.

Chantilly
Intricate floral, scallop and ribbon designs set on a fine net background.

Duchesse
Featuring floral or lace arch and scroll designs, often with raised stitching for more texture.

Guipure
Large, repetitive patterns of florals or geometrics set in circular pattern, connected by delicate threadwork.

Lyon
A lighter-weight version of Alencon, with a thinner cord.

Schiffli
A very lightweight lace with intricate embroidery, often floral, with intertwined design and connecting threading.

Spanish
Based on a standard net background featuring a rose motif.

Venice
Also known as 'Venise,' a strip of embroidery-style heavy lace not attached to netting, often in floral and geometric designs. This type of lace is often used to be cut into appliqués.

Headpieces

Backpiece
Instead of a traditional headpiece or tiara, a hair clip or comb is attached to the back of the head, and the veil is attached to that.

Bunwrap
A circular clip or band that contains hair styled into a bun, or encircles part of an up-do.

Comb
Another term for a haircomb, a simple or jeweled comb may be used as the sole hair décor, or as the attachment for a veil.

Crown
As the name implies, a small and simple or larger and more ornate, jewel-studded full crown that attaches to your head via hair combs or clips. Your personality will decide the size — small and delicate for a touch of regal look, or large and dramatic.

Half-crown
A half-circle crown of fabric-and-comb headpiece that is held in place by obscured or jeweled hairpins.

Headband
A full headwrap or slide-on clip, the headband may be solid fabric such as a shiny satin, or a pearl or crystal-adorned width.

Juliet cap
A circular cap that fits over the top of your head, either simple or adorned, worn either alone or as the attachment for a veil. The Juliet cap is named for its style reminiscent of Shakespearean plays.

Profile
A jeweled piece, much like a barrette in wide or thin design, attached appropriately to your hairstyle, most often to the side of your hair's part.

Snood
A patterned, lace or crocheted 'bun holder' that fully encases and secures an up-do.

Tapered headband
The middle of the headband is wider than the narrower ends of the headband.

Tiara
A partial crown piece affixed to the crown of the head, often held in place by combs on the sides and with additional pins. Tiaras may be thin with minimal adornment, or much larger and ornate, featuring gemstones, crystals, pearls or tiny ceramic flowers.

Wreath
A full circle made from flowers and greenery, which also may be adorned with beads and crystals.

Veils

Ballet
Falls to a length between the knee and the ankle, providing great movement.

Blusher
This is a single layer, shorter veil that is worn over the face during the ceremony, and then flipped back over the head after the ceremony. It can be worn alone and then removed after the ceremony, or paired as a layer to a longer veil.

Cathedrale
The most formal style of veil, cathedrale is usually paired with a cathedrale-length train. As such, the veil extends 3 ½ yards from the headpiece, with a significant amount trailing behind you as you walk. Stylists use the word 'regal' to describe this veil.

Chapel
This formal style of veil extends 2 ½ yards from the headpiece, extending over the train.

Double-tier
Two layers of veil, one shorter length set over a longer length. This may be a combination of a blusher or fingertip and a longer veil.

Elbow
This veil extends down to your elbows, a popular look for less formal weddings where you still want the bridal touch.

Fingertip
This veil extends down to your fingertips when your arms are hanging straight. This is the most versatile and most popular veil length for its ease of mobility.

Flyaway
As a more informal style, this veil reached just down to shoulder-length or an inch or two below your shoulders.

Fountain
A gathering at the crown of the head, creating a cascading effect around the face. This veil is most often seen in shoulder- or elbow-length to maximize volume, but may also be created in fingertip length.

Mantilla
This Spanish-style of evil is traditionally circular in shape, made of lace, tulle or chiffon, and is most often worn draped over the head, clipped into place at the temples with jeweled pins or combs, cascading elegantly over the shoulders and down the back. Modern style include a tulle or chiffon veil with intricate lace designs around the edges, and the length may extend to cathedrale length as well.

Pouf
The pouf veil is made from a gathering of veil material where it connects to the headpiece, creating a natural 'pouf' to the shoulder-length veil. Stylists use the word 'playful' to describe this veil.

Waltz
Reaches from your headpiece to the hem of your dress.

Gloves

Opera-length
Full-length gloves that reach from your fingertips all the way up to near your shoulder, perfect with a strapless or sleeveless dress. May be plain or in 6-, 8- or 10-button lengths as accents up the arm.

Elbow-length
Reaching from your fingertips to just above or just below your elbow.

Wrist-length
Reaching from your fingertips to just above or just below your wrist.

Open finger-gloves
These come in any length as mentioned above, but your fingers are exposed. Most often, the glove attaches via a ring on your middle finger, to provide the smooth silk or lace covering of the glove with full use of your fingers for the ring exchange and handling the candle taper, or signing a Ketubah, etc.

Opera-length
A full, long glove that extends to the top or middle of the upper arm, most often with 12-16 buttons.

Short
The end of the glove is two inches above the wrist, also called a 'one-button glove.'

Additional Gown Elements

Appliques
Fabric or lace cut-outs affixed to the gown, train or veil.

Beading
Refers to the embellishments created by gluing or sewing crystals, bugle beads, pearls, gemstones or other accents onto the bodice, hems or other elements of the ensemble.

Border trim
Embellishments added to bodice edges, straps, and hems, in ruffled, scalloped or braided designs.

Bustle
Gathering the train up to attach securely via obscured clips or hooks at the back of the dress, to present an attractive gathered effect above the gown's skirt.

Crinoline
The layers of tulle or netting worn under the gown's top layers to add extra volume to a full skirt. Crinoline may be attached to the dress, or added as a separate undergarment.

Edging
A narrow trim for hems, straps or veils, created from lace, embroidery, beading, or other accents.

Embroidery
Hand- or machine-stitched decorative designs created on the gown, bodice, train, or veil. Patterns vary from straight lines to intricate designs.

Paillettes
In the sequin family, paillettes are larger round accents sewn on fabric at the top and dangling to provide movement.

Ruching
Gathers or pleats in fabric, often seen at the waistline.

Seed pearls
Tiny real pearls used to embellish gowns, trains, veils and other elements. Pearls in irregular shapes are called baroque pearls.

Shirring
Fabric that has been gathered up into 3 or more parallel lines, often extending down vertically under a waistline, or used as accent on shoulder straps.

Just for laughs . . .

If you come out of the dressing room wearing a dress and one or more people laugh, do not buy it.

If one of your bridesmaids doesn't like her dress, then you are not a normal bridal party.

Weddings take place in a church because we need to pray that everything is going to work out.

Always remember, the things that go wrong will be the things you will remember and laugh about later.

Select a wedding gown for the moment that your future husband first sees it and says "Wow."

Just learning the names of the fabrics is like going back to school and learning a new vocabulary.

You know you're trouble when your mother says "Whatever you like dear, is fine with me."

I never knew that there were forty-seven different varieties of blue.

Reaching the boiling point when shopping comes in two varieties: the very loud and the very quiet.

If it feels uncomfortable when you first try it on, know it only gets worse.

Shopping with a committee does the complete opposite of what you were hoping it to do.

It's written in the Great Book that two of your bridesmaids will gain weight before the dress comes in.

Always remember that one of your bridesmaids doesn't want to be there — the problem is they never tell you.

I swear sizes were created just to depress you.

Why can't a manufacturer put a size 10 tag on a size 14 — it would make a lot of people much happier.

Why is it called alterations — in my bridal party it could have been called reconstruction.

If I wear a low cut wedding gown my future husband will love it, but my future mother-in-law will hate it ... what's a bride to do?

It's so nice to be daddy's little girl even if I am a size 16.

Is there a person who specializes in creating names for colors?

When your future mother-in-law says to you "no problem, dear" there is a problem.

When the salesperson says "we can let it out" compliment her because she could have said "go on a diet and exercise."

Sticker shock is not only the price of a dress it's the size of the dress.

If planning a wedding were so easy women wouldn't wait until after they have kids to get married.

If a bride is a princess and the groom is a prince what's your future mother-in-law?

If your fairy godmother appears at your wedding that means your wedding planner messed up.

A wedding planner is the person who is to worry about everything . . . it makes your job easier because all you have to do is worry about the wedding planner.

If you think shopping for bridesmaids dresses is bad — think about the depression when shopping for a bathing suit.

They say shopping is cheaper than a psychiatrist but after shopping for bridesmaids dresses you will need a psychiatrist.

Fashion law: if the shoe fits it's ugly.

Index

*To be a fashionable woman is to know
yourself, know what you represent, and
know what works for you. To be "in fashion"
could be a disaster on 90 percent of the
women. You are not a page out of Vogue.*

*There is
no remedy
for love
but to
love more.*

THOREAU

Apache Wedding Blessing

Now you will feel no rain
For each of you will be shelter to the other.
Now each of you will feel no cold
For each of you will be warmth to the other.
Now there is no loneliness for you
For each of you will be companion to the other.
Now you are two persons
But there is one life before you.
Go now to your dwelling place to enter into the
days of your togetherness
And may your days be good and long
upon the earth.

www.ingramcontent.com/pod-product-compliance
Lightning Source LLC
Chambersburg PA
CBHW031512270326
41930CB00006B/381